Where did you change?

A LIGHT LOOK AT

BATHING MACHINES

By Mary and David Schaefer

ISBN 0-9648692-2-5

copyright © 2006 by Mary and David Schaefer

All rights reserved

MICA PUBLISHERS

P.O. Box 1594

Bethany Beach, DE 19930

BOOK DESIGN & PAGE LAYOUT
BY JILL FEUK

Acknowledgements

Maxine Schaefer's enthusiasm for, and fascination with, bathing machines contributed in great measure to the birth of this book. Many individuals on both sides of the Atlantic have provided encouragement and assistance. Among these are Edward Wakeling, Claire and August Imholtz, Ivor Wynne Jones, Diane Cosenza, Christina Bjork, Selwyn Goodacre, Myra and Alan White, Jules and Chris Gurney, Jack Wawrzewski, Tim Bell, Marie Barnes and Liesbeth and George Blundell.

3

$\mathcal{T}$he 2007 bather shouts at the 1907
bather "where did you change".
The answer is "right here
in this little wooden box on wheels.
It's a "**bathing machine**!"
These portable bath houses came into
being in England in the early 1700's
and their use quickly spread
beyond the British Isles.
Why a "machine"? Coaches, carts and
other conveyances with wheels
were called "machines"
in the eighteenth century,
therefore a conveyance used for bathing
was called a "**bathing machine**".

It's the summer of 1875
and you're on holiday on the English Channel.
You spot this in your "Stranger's Guide":

Brighton;
STRANGER'S GUIDE

WITH ILLUSTRATIONS,

This account of Brighton would be incomplete without some mention of the conveniences for bathing. Several separate sets of machines for ladies, and others for gentlemen are stationed along the beach from Brunswick Terrace to Kemp Town. But while mentioning this fact, it will be proper to caution visitors that plunging into the sea should be considered as a medical agent, only to be employed under proper direction. The abuse of bathing is a fruitful source of disease, and not unfrequently the cause of death. Young ladies, especially, and all persons of delicate health, should be warned never to resort to sea-bathing without the permission of some medical man on the spot, and never to be tempted to remain in the water beyond a reasonable time.

and despite all this
you decide on a dip in the sea!

$\mathcal{B}$ut where do you change?
You need to rent a **bathing machine**
And here they are...

Bognor: Bathing Scene.

*M*achines
for ladies and gentlemen
are located on
separate sections of the beach.

*C*hildren change with the ladies.

*D*ouble bathing machines
are sometimes available.

$\mathcal{T}$oo shy to be seen entering the water? There may be an old machine available with a "modesty hood."

*O*n to the ticket office...

Fares for one person - Sixpence for forty minutes of usage. Threepence for each additional person.
(With inflation six pence equals about a pound in 2006, or around two US dollars).

FOLLOW THE YOUNG LADY, MAN

*P*ay and you are good to go!

Climb aboard!

*A*nd while your horse pulls you out to sea...

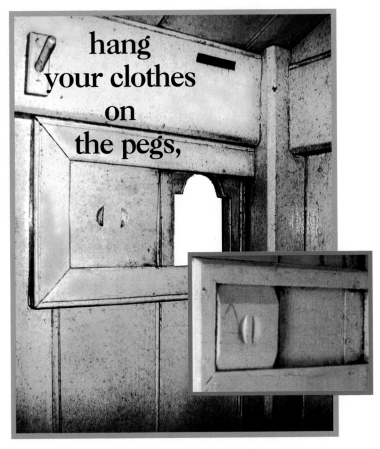

hang
your clothes
on
the pegs,

close the window for privacy,

use the mirror,

COULISSES

and emerge looking like this...

or this.

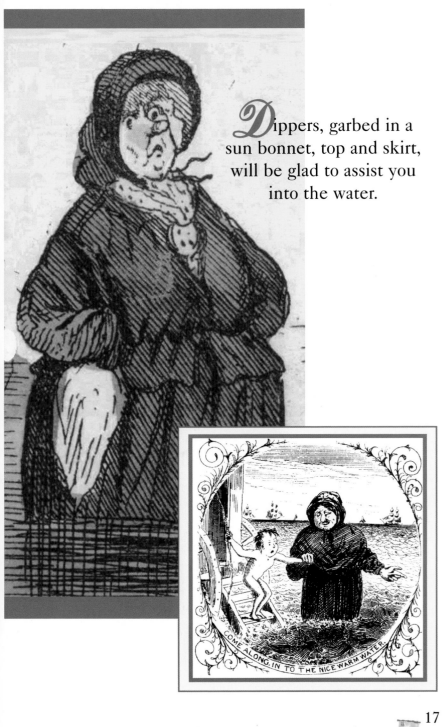

Dippers, garbed in a sun bonnet, top and skirt, will be glad to assist you into the water.

COME ALONG IN TO THE NICE WARM WATER

*S*hould you be timid she may help
you get wet by dunking you.

*B*e sure to leave your dipper a healthy tip!

*B*et you didn't know that while you were in your machine things were not going well across the Channel in Boulogne.

The tide rose over 6 feet in ten minutes at Boulogne on Saturday August 21st , threatening nearly two hundred machines and their bathers. Life-boat horns sounded for assistance and spectators volunteered their help. Handkerchiefs were waved and piteous cries for assistance emanated from the machines. Horses were pressed into service from passing omnibuses and cabs. Empty machines, rocked by the in-coming tide, floated in the water, their sides or wheels uppermost.

There was no loss of life or serious injury. On Sunday there was nothing to show where such an exciting scene occurred.

Illustrated London News,
Sept 4, 1875

**THE QUEEN'S
BATHING MACHINE**

*P*erhaps
Queen Victoria was
bathing at Osborne House
(her summer residence) on the
Isle of Wight at the same time you were
bathing at Brighton. Her bathing machine needs no horse to go
to sea. Its huge wheels run on stone rails and is lowered and
raised to and from the sea by a winch. Conveniently her
machine contains a WC!

On July 30 1847 she wrote in her diary:

*Drove down to the beach with my maids and went into the
bathing machine, where I undressed and bathed in the sea
(for the first time in my life), a very nice bathing woman
attending me. I thought it delightful until I put my head
under the water when I thought I would be stifled.*

The King

The Band

Royal Dipping, J. Nixon

Royal Dipping.

*B*ut Victoria is a latecomer to royal bathing machine use. On July 7, 1789, King George III became the first English monarch to use a bathing machine. The town band waded out and, at the moment of the royal immersion, struck up the national anthem. On July 9th the Gazette reported that the King "since he bathed, has found his health considerably improved."

*H*ad enough of the water?

Raise a flag to signal that you need a horse to haul you back to the beach.

Arrive fully dressed.

But don't let this happen to you!

Now it's time for browsing and shopping
on the ocean promenade.

*B*uy a postcard....

*P*urchase a souvenir
plate. They're great
for tea goodies...

or crested china
emblazoned with your home town crest

and some advice about when
to go bathing.

$\mathscr{H}$ow about a stereo picture to use in your stereoscope ?

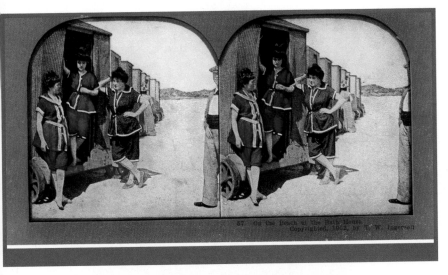

57. On the Beach at the Bath House.
Copyrighted, 1902, by T. W. Ingersoll

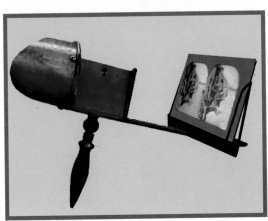

*S*hopping
is great,
but don't forget
to end your
day at the beach
with a
little romance.

*Travel next summer –
to America and change in a bathing machine
at Newport Rhode Island*

or go to Russia
and there find the little wooden boxes.

$\mathscr{P}$erhaps you will be at Ostend in Belgium

or Antwerp.

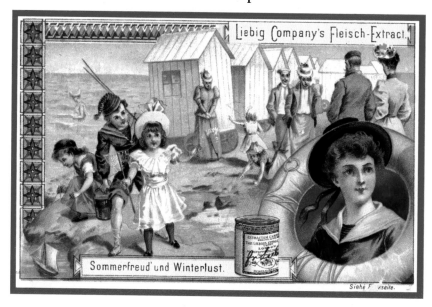

*L*ido in Italy – looks very interesting.

LIDO - VENEZIA - *Stabilimento Bagni*

*H*alfway around the world in Australia your machine comes equipped with a shark guard !

*B*ack in England you won't be able to buy
this postcard until around 1900.
The beaches are becoming "mixed" and
your whole family can bathe together.

*I*n 1735 you could have changed in this very first bathing machine on the beach at Scarborough.

*T*wo centuries later it is still not too late to change in a bathing machine - here on the Isle of Wight in 1935.

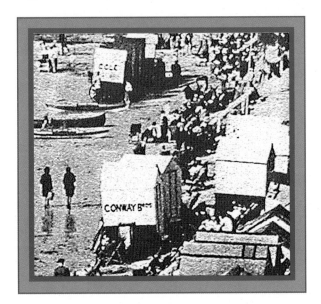

*A*nd even in 1946 at Cromer machines
are still waiting for you.

By courtesy of the Artist

*B*ut most of the little wooden boxes
entered their retirement years
well before 1940.
Now in retirement, they can still be found,
even in the 21st century, albeit
in locations other than on the shore.

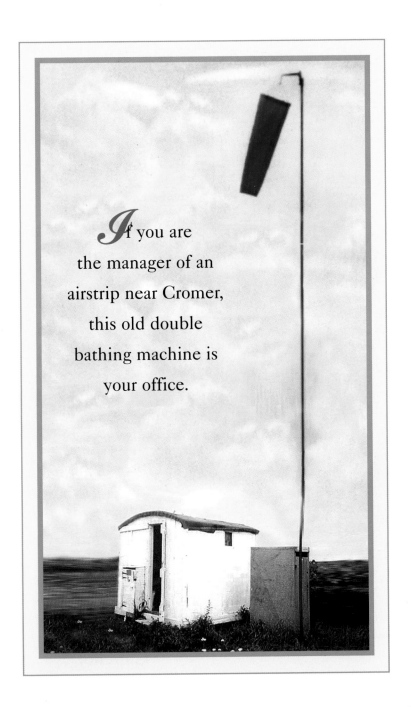

*I*f you are
the manager of an
airstrip near Cromer,
this old double
bathing machine is
your office.

*B*efore
the Euro
you could find
bathing
machines
on Belgium
Currency.

It's a lovely day for a swim — but watch out for caterpillars, snails and stinging nettles if you step out of the Victorian bathing hut on Eastbourne Allotments. Gardener Joan Hughes borrowed a navy blue and lace trimmed Victorian bathing costume and startled next door gardener Ken Turner, who took time out from tending his cabbages and carrots to pose with our bathing beauty. A neighboring gardener reminisced. 'It was my father who told me about them,* he said. 'In the 1920s the corporation sold [bathing machines] for five shillings apiece to the allotment holders [to be used as garden sheds], and they were delivered. "When I was a boy there were loads of them of course. They*ve all rotted away and gone now, except one or two."

*H*ere is what happened to another
Eastbourne tool shed

THE LANGHAM HOTEL
BATHING MACHINE
HOUNSOM'S No.49

RESCUED FROM A GARDEN ALLOTMENT AND RESTORED IN 2000.
No. 49 IS THE LAST OF HUNDREDS OF BATHING MACHINES

NOW RESTORED TO FULL WORKING ORDER
IT WAS ORIGINALLY OPERATED ON EASTBOURNE BEACH
IN THE LATE 19TH CENTURY BY Mr. HOUNSOM.

SEA BATHING BECAME POPULAR FOLLOWING A ROYAL EXAMPLE,
AND BATHING FROM MACHINES DECLINED WHEN SEGREGATED
BATHING ENDED IN 1900.

*H*ouses have been built on this former allotment at Seaford. The lonely machine has a new, if somewhat incongruous, home in the moat of the Martello fortification tower at Seaford (built to repel an attack by Napoleon on England) - now the town museum.

$\mathcal{T}$he granddaughter of Fredrick Jenkins (the builder of the machine) used number 23 as a decoration in her garden until she chose to donate it to the Bognor Regis museum in 1991.

$\mathcal{I}$n 2004 it was being lovingly restored.

$\mathcal{P}$erhaps you will be able to find
Jenkins 23 fully assembled and waiting for you
to view it in all its past splendor.

$\mathcal{B}$ut don't
try to change
in it!

FINIS!
(THE END OF THE SEASON)

SOURCES

Cover – Composite of Early 1900's postcard and modern photograph by authors.
Back Cover – T shirt design by Diane Cosenza

Page 5 –   Brighton: Stranger's Guide, circa 1870, page 80.

Page 6 –   Bottom – Collection of Towner Art Gallery and Museum, Eastbourne.

Page 7 –   Bottom – Rhyl, portion of postcard in collection of
The National Library of Wales, Aber ystwyth.

Page 8 –   Bottom – Detail from photograph of Ventnor, circa 1895.

Page 9 –   Bottom – Image of machine from collection of Cromer Museum, Cromer.

The images at the top of pages 10 and 17 are from: *Mr. Perri Winks'
Submarine Adventure & Dream at Sea*, A yarn spun by T. Onwhyn,
Kershaw & Son, London, 1890's.

Page 10 –   Bottom – Punch, or the London Charivari, October 1, 1870.

The cartoons on the bottom of pages 11 and 17 are from *Recollections
of the Sea Side*, a miniature panorama, Newman & Co.,London, 1860's.

The fares on page 11 are from *Bye-Laws for the Regulation of
Bathing Machines*, Llandudno Wales, 1868.

Photographic images on pages 12, 13, 26, 36, 40 (bottom) and 42
are from photographs by the authors taken at Bognor Regis,
Seaford and Cromer.

Page 13 –   Top – The Illustrated London News, November 29, 1879.
Colored by authors.

Page 14 –   La vie d'Ostende, Ostend 1896. Part of illustration entitled
DÂ´eesses du bain.

Page 15 –   Cartoon cira 1800 reproduced on cover of History Today, July 1983.

Page 16 –   The Sketch, Sept. 8, 1897.

Page 18 –   George Cruikshank engraving, pre 1878.

Page 19 and 20 – Illustrated London News, Sept 4, 1875.

Page 21 –   Line image from Osborne House coloring card.

Page 22 –   Engraving by John Nixon.

Page 23 –   Middle – Photograph by Paul Martin, an early British photographer,
using a camera called the "FacileHand Camera" during the summer
of 1892. Used with permission from Victoria & Albert Museum.

Page 23 – Bottom – Mr. Punch at the Seaside, N.D.(circa 1880), page 186. The drawing is entitled *The Disorder of the Bath*. Caption: How Belinda Brown appeared with "waves all over her hairbefore taking a bath in the sea. – and – How she looked after having some more "waves all over it".

Page 24, 28, & 32 – Postcards.

Page 25 – Contemporary plate owned by authors.

Page 26 – Crested China bathing machines in authors collection. Manufactured circa 1910. Top photograph by Ephraim Salins.

Page 27 – Stereoscopic card, *On the beach at the Bath House*, copyright 1902 by T. W. Ingersoll.

Page 29 – Top – From the collection of the Newport Historical Society. Mid 1870's photo.

Page 29 – Bottom – *"Sestroretsk Beach on the bank of the Gulf of Finland"* pre 1910. St. Petersburg: Capital of the Russian Empire.

Page 30 – Top – Internet Image from Museo Dei Bagni Di Mare, http://www.balnea.net

Page 31 – Bottom – Internet image, http://www.personal.usyd.edu.au

Page 33 – Top – 1735 engraving by John Setterington.

Page 33 – Bottom – National Geographic Magizine, Jan 1935, Page 29.

Page 34 – Painting by Robert Greenham.

Page 36 – The Belgium One Hundred Frank note was issued to honor artist James Ensor.

Page 37 – Photograph T. Conno ly and text (condensed) by D. Mulley. Eastbourne Herald 1989. Used w th the kind permission of the Eastbourne Herald and Gazette.

Page 38 – Internet image.

Page 40 – Top – Photo from Bognor Regis Observer, March 14, 1991. Used with the kind permission of the Bognor Regis Observer.

Page 42 – Mr. Punch at the Seaside, page 191.